# Understanding Disease and Disorders

# Phobias

## Gail B. Stewart

**KIDHAVEN PRESS**
*An imprint of Thomson Gale, a part of The Thomson Corporation*

Detroit • New York • San Francisco • San Diego • New Haven, Conn. • Waterville, Maine • London • Munich

On cover: Some phobias cause people to be so fearful of the world
that they find it hard to leave home.

*For more information, contact*
KidHaven Press
27500 Drake Rd.
Farmington Hills, MI 48331-3535
Or you can visit our Internet site at http://www.gale.com

**LIBRARY OF CONGRESS CATALOGING-IN-PUBLICATION DATA**

Gail B. Stewart.
  Phobias / by Gail B. Stewart.
    v. cm. — (Understanding diseases and disorders)
  Includes bibliographical references and index.
    Contents: An overpowering fear—Where do phobias come from?—Living with
a phobia—Overcoming phobias.
    ISBN 0-7377-2169-3 (hbk. : alk. paper)
    I. Title. II. Series. (San Diego, Calif.)

Printed in the United States of America

# Contents

## Chapter One

# An Overpowering Fear

Fourteen-year-old Jamie cannot help his father in the garden because he is afraid of snakes. He is not sure why, he says, but even seeing one on television gives him the creeps. "It doesn't matter that they aren't poisonous," he says. "Knowing that they can't hurt me doesn't help. Just knowing they are out there scares me. I think about them slithering around my feet. That's the worst! I've even had nightmares about snakes."[1]

Jamie says that no one else in his family shares his fear. "I get teased by my sisters a lot," he admits. "But I can't help it. I think about snakes and I get nervous. Just talking about them—even that's hard."[2]

He says that at first his parents thought he was pretending to be afraid just to get out of doing garden work. "But they understand now," he says. "I told them I'd do any other chore—cleaning the bathrooms, anything—just so I wouldn't have to be out in the garden. I don't mind bugs or mice or anything else," he adds. "Just snakes."[3]

## "I'd Get an F"

Martha, age thirteen, has a fear, too. "I'm afraid of talking in front of people, like in a group. I can talk to one person at a time, or maybe two. That's okay—I don't get scared if it's just a couple of people.

**The idea of a snake encounter can be paralyzing to a person with a snake phobia.**

"But if I have to give a report or something at school, I freeze up. I can't talk, and I feel like I am going to faint in front of everyone. Last year in science class, I had to present my science project in front of my class, and I couldn't even talk. I was shaking and I felt like my heart was beating faster than it was possible for a heart to beat.

"I thought I would maybe faint, or throw up, or something really awful. I couldn't even get one word out—it was like being in the worst bad dream you could think of. I just left the room and went to the bathroom. I was so embarrassed—but

**A student who has an extreme fear of speaking in front of classmates might choose a failing grade rather than give an oral report.**

I knew it would be like that. I just knew. But anyway, that's how scary it is for me."[4]

Martha insists that she is not shy. "It's not the same as being shy. It's way worse than shy. It's hard to explain if you never felt that way. One of my friends says I'm just being a baby, but I'm not. I'm just too afraid, and I guess if people don't understand, that's too bad. I told my mom that next time I have to do something like give a report or something, I'm staying home. I won't do it. Even if the teacher told me I'd get an F, I still couldn't do it."[5]

## "The Worst Feeling in the World"

The sensation Jamie and Martha feel is much more than simply being afraid of something. Each of them suffers from a **phobia**, or a fear that is so intense it is unreasonable for the situation. If threatened by a poisonous snake, for example, it would be reasonable for anyone to feel fear. However, it is unreasonable for a person to feel fear when talking about snakes or seeing a snake on television. There is no reason to feel fear in those situations, because there is no threat.

Martha's fear is too intense for the situation too. It would be perfectly reasonable for her to feel a little nervous before a school report. Many people about to speak in front of a group experience twinges of nervousness—sometimes called "butterflies." But that nervousness usually goes away once they begin talking.

Because Martha says that she would rather risk a failing grade and stay home than give a report in class, her fear is unreasonable. "My mom says everyone gets nervous," says Martha. "But not everyone gets light-headed, and [gets] a pounding heart like I do—just thinking about it. It's the worst feeling in the world."[6]

Feeling such intense fear toward snakes or speaking in front of people is not a normal reaction, but Jamie and Martha are certainly not alone. Psychologists—people who study human behavior—say that phobias affect as many as 26 million people in the United States. That makes phobias the number one mental health disorder in the nation—more common than depression or substance abuse.

## Various Types

Phobias are broken into three basic groups. **Specific phobias** are fears of particular things. A fear of cats is a specific phobia, as is a fear of lightning. Experts say there are hundreds of specific things for which people have phobias. Some are fairly common, such as fear of a type of animal or a fear of heights.

There are also phobias that are much more unusual, such as the fear of bare toes or the fear of the number eight. One psychologist says she has

A fear of cats or other types of animals is fairly common.

talked with someone who is deathly afraid of cucumbers. Washington, D.C., phobia expert Jerilyn Ross knew a woman who was afraid of anything having to do with Wisconsin. "She wouldn't go into a supermarket," says Ross, "unless her husband went in first and checked out where all the cheeses came from."[7]

No matter how strange sounding, however, phobias are no laughing matter to those who suffer from them. Jane, a fifty-four-year-old history teacher, has been terrified of clowns as long as she can remember. "My friends all know about it," she says. "And I get kidded all the time—even the kids I teach say, 'How can anyone get scared of clowns?' I can't explain it. I know it sounds funny, especially because I'm a grown woman. But it isn't a joke to me."[8]

A person with a fear of heights would not be able to stand on, or look down from, a high building ledge.

# The Most Common Fears

While people with a specific phobia are afraid of a certain animal or thing, those with a **social phobia** are afraid of how other people might react to them. Social phobias are the most common fears of all. In fact, psychologists estimate that between 7 and 10 percent of people in the United States have a social phobia.

Many people, like Martha, fear speaking in public. Others worry about eating in front of other people, or about blushing. One young woman says she was so fearful of walking down the aisle in front of hundreds of guests, she almost dreaded her wedding day. Candy, another woman, says she was afraid of writing checks in stores because people could see how her hands tremble. "It happened once, and that was enough," she says. "I was shaking so much, I don't know how they could even read my writing."[9]

## "It's a Terrible Way to Live"

While specific and social phobias can be real problems, experts agree that there is one phobia that is more frightening—and its symptoms more serious—than any other. Called **agoraphobia**, or fear of public places, it can make people afraid to go to restaurants, grocery stores, or malls. It can make it difficult for a person to ride a bus or a train. Some people with agoraphobia

# Three Major Types of Phobias

**Specific phobia:** An intense, unreasonable fear of specific objects or situations.

**Social phobia:** An extreme fear of being embarrassed in social situations.

**Agoraphobia:** An intense fear of public places.

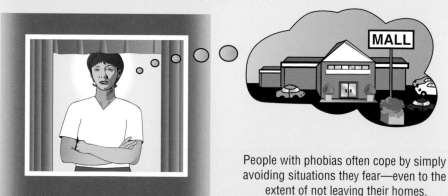

People with phobias often cope by simply avoiding situations they fear—even to the extent of not leaving their homes.

are so afraid they cannot even leave their own homes.

"I have had agoraphobia for years," says one woman. "And it has been the hardest part of my life. I am limited in what I can do, and I have missed so many things. I'm not homebound like some [people with agoraphobia are], but there are days when the idea is tempting. I'm not really comfortable for long anyplace but home. It's a terrible way to live."[10]

## Chapter Two

# Where Do Phobias Come From?

**S**ince ancient times, phobias have puzzled doctors. They have wondered what causes phobias and why some people have phobias while others do not. Through the centuries, doctors and psychologists have come up with theories about the cause of certain fears.

## Some Simple Answers

Psychologists used to believe that all phobias were caused by a bad experience. Someone who had been bitten by a cat, for example, might develop a cat phobia. Someone else who as a child was caught in a bad storm might develop a fear of thunder and lightning later in life.

This theory applies to many phobias. One woman who once had a phobia about eating in front of other people says that she knows where her fear came from.

"I was twelve. I had gone to my friend Ruthie's house for lunch. For one reason or another, I felt sick to my stomach after eating, and I thought I might be going to throw up. Ruthie was talking to her mom upstairs, and I couldn't remember where the bathroom was. I didn't know what to do—I was running around downstairs looking and all of a sudden, I threw up in the hallway. Oh, I was so embarrassed!

**People who suffer from social phobias may have difficulty with commonplace activities such as eating in public.**

"Ruthie's mom reassured me. She said it wasn't my fault. But I still felt awful, and I never wanted to go anywhere to eat except home. I never ate in restaurants, or at birthday parties. That lasted more than ten years! It was a very stressful part of my life, and I have many bad memories of that time. I felt so different from my friends, you know?"[11]

## Not Always a Simple Answer

While some phobias can be traced back to a specific experience, this is not always the case. For example, this theory does not explain why some people who have been bitten by a cat develop a phobia while others do not.

Mia, a college sophomore, was thrown from a horse when she was ten. "I broke my collarbone and two teeth got knocked out," she says. "I never was afraid of horses before my accident, and I wasn't afraid after being thrown. I was a little nervous about riding again, I admit, but it went okay. I don't have a horse phobia. I love horses."[12]

The "bad experience" theory also does not explain phobias that occur in people who cannot recall ever having a bad experience with the feared thing.

Greta, who has always lived in the city, does have a fear of horses. She has never ridden a horse and has only seen horses from a distance. Yet she has a severe fear of horses. In fact, she can barely

Some people have no fear of horses, even after a fall. Horse phobics fear even the idea of touching a horse.

talk about horses without shuddering. "I don't know why I'm afraid of them," she says. "But there is *nothing* that could make me go near a horse!"[13]

## A Different Theory

In the early 1920s, a psychologist named John B. Watson came up with a theory of his own about fears. He set out to see if phobias could be learned at a very young age. If so, he reasoned that might explain why some people did not recall an unpleasant experience with the thing they feared. Perhaps, he suggested, they did have an experience, but they were just too young to remember.

John B. Watson concluded that phobias were learned at a very young age.

Watson's experiments centered around an eleven-month-old baby named Albert. Albert was a happy, easygoing baby who did not seem to be afraid of anything except loud noises (as all babies are). He liked to play with the animals in Watson's laboratory—a dog, a rabbit, and a white rat.

Watson wanted to see if he could "teach" Albert to have a phobia. He watched while Albert played. Whenever the baby touched the rat, Watson banged an iron bar above Albert's head. The loud noise startled him, and he screamed and cried. Watson repeated the experiment over and over. Soon Albert began to associate, or link, the scary noise and the rat. Whenever the rat was brought close to him, the baby showed intense fear. Albert had learned a phobia, as Watson predicted.

## "Tagalong Fears"

After finishing his experiment, Watson made a surprising discovery. Albert had developed not only a phobia of white rats, but also of other things that were white and furry like the rat. Without meaning to, Watson had given Albert what some referred to as "tagalong fears," or phobias of things that looked like the rat. Although he had never feared them before, Albert had also learned to fear things such as cotton balls, toy rabbits, and even a Santa Claus mask with a white beard.

Many psychologists found Watson's work fascinating. It was interesting, they felt, that phobias could begin in infancy. It was also interesting that a phobia learned at a young age might be a "tagalong," or something that in some way resembled the original fear. This would make it even more difficult to trace the origin of phobias.

Other psychologists were critical of Watson's work. They pointed out that Watson worked with only one child. They did not think that was enough evidence to make any conclusions about phobias. Other ideas about phobias were presented over the years, but no one answer was ever agreed on—at least for most phobias.

## Looking at Agoraphobia

Experts have had more success finding the cause of agoraphobia, the fear of public places. They say that this phobia begins with a very scary episode called a panic attack. Panic attacks are believed to be the highest level of fear or anxiety a human can feel. Researchers are not certain why some people have such attacks, but they believe something may be wrong with the body's chemistry. No one can predict who will suffer a panic attack or in what circumstances.

Carrie, a college student, had a panic attack when she was a senior in high school. At the time, she did not understand what was happening to her.

"My lips got numb. My heart was beating so fast and I was breathing—gasping—faster than I ever knew I could breathe. It was so scary, I can't even explain.

"I mean, I thought I was going to have a stroke or a heart attack or something. And I hadn't even been doing anything strenuous, you know? I wasn't stressed out—before the panic attack, that is. I was just walking into the mall—I hadn't even gone into one store. And I had to run out of there, back to my car."[14]

Other people who have had panic attacks say the same things. Many assume they are having a medical problem such as a heart attack. Often people go to a hospital, fearing they will die. Another young panic attack victim says he worried that he had lost his mind. He ran out of a store as he struggled to breathe and catch his breath. "I ran for the nearest outdoor exit and pushed through the doors," he says. "There I stayed, plastered to

**During a panic attack, a person might experience a sudden surge of overwhelming fear.**

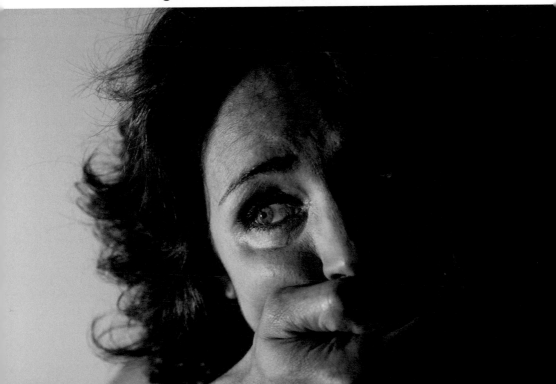

a bench, staring at the sky, taking slow deep breaths and wondering if I was going insane."[15]

## Avoiding Panic

Once the panicked person's heart and breathing slow down, the panicky feeling goes away. But often what replaces it is a phobia. He or she develops a fear of panic attacks and worries that another one will occur. "I had never felt that way," says Anne, who experienced a panic attack while driving. "And I didn't feel that I could live through another one. I told myself, if I stay out of my car, I'll be fine."[16]

Psychologists say that linking the fear of a panic attack to whatever one was doing at the time of suffering one is the beginning of agoraphobia.

Everything swirls and feels confused to someone having a panic attack in a crowded mall.

Carrie stopped going to the mall after suffering a panic attack there. "I stayed out of the mall," she says. "I just stopped shopping, or if I did go, I'd run into a regular store I could get in and out of really fast."[17] Other people might stop driving or stay away from concerts. Gradually, they limit the places they can go without worrying about a panic attack.

One young mother experienced a second panic attack and decided she would stop leaving the house. "It wasn't long before I was staying home all day, every day," she says. "That's where I felt the safest, and that's what I had to do. It was survival."[18] Her fear of panic attacks had become a severe case of agoraphobia.

## A Point of Agreement

There are hundreds of phobias. While some may be explained by panic attacks or a frightening experience, others are mysteries. Some experts feel that certain people may be more likely to have phobias because they tend to be more anxious. Some believe that people may inherit the tendency to get phobias.

Psychologists do not agree on what causes phobias. One thing they do agree on, however, is that life with a phobia can be very challenging. Unless someone has had a phobia, or knows someone who does, it is hard to understand how difficult life can be when one is afraid.

## Chapter Three

# Living with a Phobia

Just as phobias vary, their effects on individuals vary, too. Some people find themselves crippled by their fears. Not a day goes by when they are able to live a normal life. On the other hand, millions of people have found that they can avoid fear only by making changes in the way they live.

## Limiting Careers

It is common for people with phobias to change the type of work they do. For example, Madeline had a teaching job in a rural area and suddenly developed a phobia about driving her car. She was worried because she had no other way to get to school. "I couldn't carpool, since no other teachers lived near me," she says. "I thought I might have to quit my teaching job, and that really worried me. I'd waited so long to be a teacher, and I was really discouraged."[19]

She decided to take another teaching job—in the city. "I could take a bus," she explains. "It wasn't a perfect solution. I missed the kids in my other school, and my new job didn't pay as well. But at least I was able to keep teaching, and that was the main thing."[20]

Fear of flying creates job difficulties, too. One man says he became afraid to fly just six months

**A person who fears flying is more concerned about what might happen than with what is actually happening on the plane.**

after being hired for a job he had always wanted. "It was pretty bad," he says. "I had the job of my dreams, but [the phobia] ended all that. I developed a really strong fear of flying. I couldn't make myself get on an airplane. I don't know where the phobia came from, but it brought my career to a standstill. I'd always been in sales, but in this business, you've got to fly."[21]

His story is not uncommon. One New York **therapist** says the fear can be so strong that not even a big pay raise can tempt someone with a flying phobia. "Many [patients] will not fly even when they're offered triple their salary,"[22] he says.

## "I Couldn't Do It"

Patty's phobia of speaking in front of other people forced her to change directions, too. She had planned on studying English in college. "That changed," she says. "I'd already done three semesters and then I realized I had to take a speech class. There was no way I could talk in front of the class. And it wasn't just one speech. I think you had to give maybe five or six during the semester. I couldn't do it."[23]

Ron's **claustrophobia**, or fear of small spaces, is what has made his job difficult. Ron says the biggest problem with his phobia is that he cannot make himself ride an elevator. "I panic," he explains. "I can't do it. I see the doors start to close and I feel like I'm going to be trapped. I even have trouble breathing."[24]

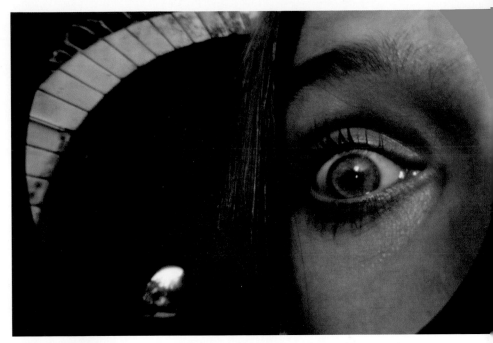

Fear of being in a tunnel, or in other enclosed spaces, is called claustrophobia.

As a result, Ron must use the stairs at work and at his apartment building. "I used to work in an office on the twelfth floor," he says, "and that was too high. I was so tired from climbing up twelve flights of stairs that I got a different job—a lower one!"[25]

## Dangerous Phobias

Some phobias can affect more than a person's job. They can lead to physical problems, too. There are many people whose fear of doctors keeps them from getting checkups when they should. Some say that even the smell of a doctor's office frightens them.

A phobia about doctors can be dangerous because it could lead a person to avoid checkups, inoculations, or hospitals.

"I used to get my hair cut in the same building where lots of doctors have offices," says John, who has a fear of shots. "But I stopped going there. There was that smell, you know? I don't know if it's the antiseptic or what, but it didn't agree with me. I go to the barbershop on the other end of town now. That way, I don't have to be reminded about going to the doctor."[26]

Dental phobias are common, too. People who suffer from a fear of dentists may put off having their teeth checked for many years. As a result, they experience a great amount of pain and spend thousands of dollars to repair the damage to their teeth. "Sometimes, a patient will come in and his teeth are actually rotten," says one dental hygienist. "You feel so bad, because their fear was so strong it kept them from getting help."[27]

## "I Was Really Missing Out"

The most serious phobias are the ones that control people's lives, even when they try to make adjustments. Many people with social phobias, for instance, find themselves avoiding other people because they are so frightened. Anne says she felt torn each time friends invited her out. "Part of me wanted to go out with my friends," she says. "Part of me knew I just couldn't do it. Not in a million years; I just couldn't do it."[28]

People with severe social phobias begin to feel as though life is passing them by. They feel cut off and alone. As a result of their loneliness, many people with phobias use—and abuse—alcohol and other drugs to make themselves feel better.

Many people with agoraphobia face these problems, too. Rusty, who developed agoraphobia six years ago, says that he began to lie to people. "They'd call and say, 'Let's go to a ball game,' or 'Come on over and we'll put hamburgers on the grill,'" he says. "I was so worried about having a panic attack, I knew that was out of the question. But they didn't know about [my agoraphobia]."[29]

Rusty says he felt foolish telling his friends about his fears. Instead of telling the truth, he says, he lied to his friends. "I'd tell them I was really tired, or that I had plans with my family or something," he says. "And what happened after that was pretty predictable, right? My friends stopped calling. They just figured I wasn't interested, and stopped thinking about me. In a way I was relieved. I didn't have to think up excuses any more. But in another way, you know, it hurt. I was really missing out on things I used to enjoy."[30]

## Is There Hope?

To someone with a phobia, fear can be a way of life. "I can't even remember a time when I wasn't afraid of close spaces," says Ron. "I'm afraid, and

**People with social phobias may drink alcohol or use drugs to help them deal with social situations.**

A person with agoraphobia might stop seeing his friends because he is worried about having a panic attack.

it's something I don't forget. Not one day goes by when I forget it. I used to wish I wasn't afraid. Now I just accept it."[31]

Some experts say that people with phobias should not accept being afraid. In fact, they say, there are more and more reasons to be hopeful that even the most severe phobias can be managed or even cured completely.

## Chapter Four

# Overcoming Phobias

**N**ot everyone with a phobia seeks help. Some people are able to manage the fear by themselves, especially a specific phobia. Someone who is afraid of cats, for example, can simply avoid going to homes where there are cats. "I just ask, if it's someone I don't know," says Ben. "It's pretty easy. I just say that I'm not a cat person, so I'd prefer getting together somewhere else if they have a cat. People are usually pretty understanding."[32]

## Confronting Fears

People with more serious fears often cannot manage them alone, however. They may seek professional help from a therapist. One of the most common types of therapy today helps patients confront, or face, their worst fears. The idea behind **confrontation therapy**, as it is called, is that when people face their phobias, they usually learn that there is no real basis for fear. "If you really want to make the fear calm down," says one therapist, "you have to physically confront the thing that is scary to you. You have to actually experience it, so that you see for yourself that nothing bad happens."[33]

It is difficult to face a phobia alone. Many people seek professional help.

# Facing Fears: Confrontation Therapy

With a therapist's help, a patient confronts her phobia, fear of spiders.

*She ranks the level of fear she experiences in ten situations with spiders. Number one is the least frightening, and ten is the scariest.*

1    2    3    4    5    6    7    8    9    10

*She imagines being in the least frightening situation—looking at a picture of a spider—until it no longer causes her fear.*

*She works, in order, on imagining herself in the remaining nine situations, until the most frightening experience—holding a spider—no longer causes fear.*

*She then moves on to real life experiences for each of the ten situations, in the same order.*

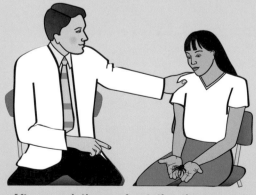

*After completing confrontation therapy, she can now hold a spider without fear.*

Usually, this type of therapy is done in stages. "I'll ask a patient to rank different aspects of the phobia from one to ten," explains one therapist. "A 10 would be the scariest, and a 1 the least. For instance, if the patient has a dog phobia, he might rank 'looking at a picture of a dog' as a 2. He'd probably assign the highest rank to 'being approached by a dog.'"[34]

Once the patient ranks each aspect, the therapist asks him or her to imagine being in the first situation—the least scary one. Once he or she can imagine that one without fear, the patient and the therapist move to the next situation. Eventually the patient can imagine even the scariest encounter without the fear.

## "Move Slowly, Don't Rush"

Once the imagining is done, the patient moves on to real exposure to the phobia. Again, the patient begins with the least scary situation and works down the list. Kris, who suffered from a severe phobia of dogs, received help from her therapist. "I did the imagining okay," she remembers, "but it was a whole different thing in real life. Dr. Lyman [her therapist] helped me with relaxed breathing, to help me when I started getting fearful. She said to just move slowly, don't rush."[35]

Kris says that she worked for months on getting rid of her phobia, and she did it. "The whole thing for me was baby steps," she says. "I never went faster than I was comfortable with. I remember walking over to a bench and sitting down near this man and his dog. That was my most scary situation, approaching a dog. When I was going to actually do it, I kept saying, 'Breathe, relax, breathe.' When I sat down, I almost cried. What a relief! It was true—nothing bad happened!"[36]

Psychologists say this is the point of confronting a phobia. "Once you see that the world doesn't come crashing down on you, it's a good feeling. For the first time in a long time, you are not being controlled by the fear. You're controlling your own feelings. To someone with a phobia, that's like being set free."[37]

## Help for Agoraphobia

The one type of phobia that is usually not helped by confrontation therapy is agoraphobia. Experts believe that the fear of having a panic attack is too crippling for most sufferers to deal with—even with gradual steps.

However, in recent years researchers have found that some medications can help. Known as **antidepressants**, these drugs can block panic attacks in many patients with agoraphobia. When a patient realizes that the threat of a panic attack is no longer there, it is easier to relax and deal with situations that are scary.

Zori, a sixty-year-old woman who suffered from agoraphobia for many years, says she had good

A boy with a deathly fear of spiders learns to overcome his fear through confrontation therapy.

results with medications. "I was so afraid of having a panic episode," she says. "But my doctor assured me I probably wouldn't have one at all. Or if I did, it would be real mild. He was right. But that wasn't the end of it. I still had to work on the fears I had built up—fear of going to movies, going to busy places, things like that."[38]

# Life Doesn't Have to Be Scary

There is still plenty about phobias that remains a mystery. The causes for a great many fears are unknown. No one understands why some people are fearful while others are not. Even so, therapists are very optimistic about the future. New developments

**Antidepressants sometimes help people with agoraphobia lead more social, happy lives.**

in medications and therapies are making life much easier for those with phobias.

"I feel like my life is my own now," says Zori. "I feel like a kid—not scared of anything. My only regret is looking back on those years of hiding out, you know? Life is a lot more fun when you can enjoy it, rather than being afraid of it."[39]

# Notes

## Chapter 1: An Overpowering Fear

1. Jamie, personal interview, Minneapolis, MN, March 3, 2004.

2. Jamie.

3. Jamie.

4. Martha, personal interview, Minneapolis, MN, March 16, 2004.

5. Martha.

6. Martha.

7. Quoted in Stephen Rae, "Who's Afraid of the Big Bad Phobia?" *Cosmopolitan*, September 1994, p. 218.

8. Jane, telephone interview, March 21, 2004.

9. Candy, telephone interview, May 28, 2000.

10. Name withheld, interview, May 15, 2000.

## Chapter 2: Where Do Phobias Come From?

11. Name withheld, interview, March 31, 2004.

12. Mia, personal interview, Minneapolis, MN, March 26, 2004.

13. Greta, telephone interview, February 28, 2004.

14. Carrie, personal interview, Richfield, MN, May 26, 2000.

15. Quoted in "When Fear Takes Control," *Teen*, January 1995, p. 25.

16. Anne, telephone interviews, June 1, 14, and 15, 2000.

17. Carrie.

18. Anne.

## Chapter 3: Living with a Phobia

19. Madeline, telephone interview, February 29, 2004.

20. Madeline.

21. Dan, personal interview, Eden Prairie, MN, May 15, 16, 2000.

22. Quoted in Garret Condon, "Getting a Fix on Fear," *Hartford Courant*, February 13, 2004, p. D1.

23. Patty, personal interview, Minneapolis, MN, March 26, 2004.

24. Ron, telephone interview, March 27, 2004.

25. Ron.

26. John, personal interview, Richfield, MN, May 28, 2000.

27. Maddie, telephone interview, May 14, 2000.

28. Anne.

29. Rusty, telephone interview, March 18, 2004.

30. Rusty.

31. Ron.

## Chapter 4: Overcoming Phobias

32. Ben, telephone interview, March 26, 2004.

33. Quoted in Condon, "Getting a Fix on Fear," p. D1.

34. Dr. Patty, personal interview, Edina, MN, March 31, 2004.

35. Kris, telephone interview, May 14, 2000.

36. Kris.

37. Dr. Patty.

38. Zori, telephone interview, March 22, 2004.

39. Zori.

# Glossary

**agoraphobia:** The fear of public places.

**antidepressant:** A medication that can fight anxiety or depression.

**claustrophobia:** The fear of small spaces.

**confrontation therapy:** Dealing with a phobia by facing the thing that is most frightening.

**phobia:** An intense, irrational fear of something.

**social phobia:** The fear of the critical reaction of other people.

**specific phobia:** The fear of a particular thing or situation.

**therapist:** A psychologist who helps people deal with problems such as phobias.

# For Further Exploration

## Books
Ada P. Kahn, *Phobias*. New York: Franklin Watts, 2003. Readable text, good information on getting rid of phobias.

Judy Monroe, *Phobias: Everything You Wanted to Know but Were Afraid to Ask*. Springfield, NJ: Enslow, 1996. Helpful glossary as well as a good list of various specific phobias.

## Periodicals
Randi Hutter Epstein, "Quick Fix Helps Ease Kids' Phobias," *Orlando Sentinel*, January 24, 2004.

Joannie M. Schrof, "Why Everyone Gets Stage Fright," *U.S. News & World Report*, June 21, 1999.

## Web Sites
**Kidshealth** (www.kidshealth.org). This Web site contains a good section on anxiety and fears common in children. Also offers good information on how parents can help children with fears.

**Royal Society of Psychiatrists** (www.rcpsych. ac.uk). Excellent graphics and cartoons depicting various situations that can result in phobias. Very readable text.

# Index

# Picture Credits

Cover image: © Royalty-Free/CORBIS
© Bruno/CORBIS, 10
© Robert Essel NYC/CORBIS, 30
© Al Francekevich/CORBIS, 9
Hulton/Archive by Getty Images, 18
© Richard Hutchings/CORBIS, 6
© Jose Luis Pelaez, Inc./CORBIS, 38
Kevin Kolczynski/Reuters/Landov, 5
© LWA-Dann Tardif, 28
© LWA-Stephen Welstead/CORBIS, 15
© Roy Morsch/CORBIS, 21
Brandy Noon, 12, 34
Photos.com, 31, 33
© Pierre Perrin/CORBIS SYGMA, 22, 27
© Royalty-Free/CORBIS, 25
© Norbert Schaefer/CORBIS, 37
© Shearer Images/CORBIS, 17

# About the Author

Gail B. Stewart received her undergraduate degree from Gustavus Adolphus College in St. Peter, Minnesota. She did her graduate work in English, linguistics, and curriculum study at the College of St. Thomas and the University of Minnesota. She taught English and reading for more than ten years.

She has written over ninety books for young people, including a series for Lucent Books called The Other America. She has written many books on historical topics such as World War I and the Warsaw ghetto.

Stewart and her husband live in Minneapolis with their three sons, Ted, Elliot, and Flynn; two dogs; and a cat. When she is not writing, she enjoys reading, walking, and watching her sons play soccer.